C++ ESSENTIALS

THE POCKET REFERENCE

Author

Debajyoti Bhattacharjee

TOPIC DISCUSSED

C++ Basics

Introduction to C++

C++ is a high-level programming language developed by Bjarne Stroustrup at Bell Labs in the early 1980s as an extension of the C programming language. Known for its efficiency, performance, and flexibility, C++ is widely used in software development for systems, applications, and games. This language introduced object-oriented programming (OOP) concepts, allowing developers to model real-world problems more effectively.

History and Features of C++

History of C++

- **1979**: Bjarne Stroustrup started developing "C with Classes" at Bell Labs, aiming to add features of Simula (an object-oriented language) to C.
- **1983**: The language was renamed to **C++**, inspired by the increment operator in C, symbolizing an extension or "increment" of C.
- **1985**: The first official version of C++ was released, with foundational support for

classes and objects, constructors, and destructors.

- **1989**: ANSI standardized C++ as the ANSI C++ language, helping unify language features across platforms.
- **1998**: The first ISO C++ standard, known as **C++98**, was published. It included the Standard Template Library (STL).
- **2011**: **C++11** introduced several new features such as auto keyword, nullptr, lambda expressions, smart pointers, and threading support.
- **2014, 2017, and 2020**: Further updates (C++14, C++17, C++20) brought more improvements in safety, readability, and performance with features like structured bindings, filesystem library, and coroutines.

Features of C++

- **Object-Oriented Programming (OOP)**: C++ supports OOP principles like encapsulation, inheritance, and polymorphism, helping in modular and reusable code development.
- **Compiled Language**: C++ is compiled, meaning it translates to machine code for faster execution, making it highly efficient.
- **Low-Level Manipulation**: C++ provides low-level access to memory through

pointers, enabling systems programming and embedded programming.

- **Standard Template Library (STL)**: STL in C++ offers reusable data structures and algorithms, like vectors, stacks, and sort functions, making development faster and more efficient.
- **Rich Library Support**: C++ has an extensive standard library for handling file I/O, data manipulation, and other common operations.
- **Multiple Paradigms**: Supports procedural, object-oriented, and even functional programming styles, offering flexibility for developers.
- **Portability**: C++ programs can run across different operating systems with minimal changes, thanks to standardized libraries and compiler support.

Differences Between C and C++

C++ is an extension of the C programming language, which means it retains many of C's features but also adds new ones, especially around OOP. Here's a comparison:

Feature	C	C++
Paradigm	Procedural Programming	Multi-Paradigm: Procedural +

		Object-Oriented
Data Encapsulation	Not Supported	Supported using Classes
Inheritance	Not Supported	Supported for code reuse
Polymorphism	Not Supported	Supported (Function and Operator Overloading)
Memory Management	Primarily manual with malloc and free	Enhanced with new and delete operators
Function Overloading	Not Supported	Supported
Namespace Support	Not Available	Available to avoid naming conflicts
Standard Library	Limited Standard Library	Extensive Standard Template Library (STL)
Exception Handling	Basic error handling via return codes	Structured exception handling with try-catch
Applications	Low-level systems and hardware	General-purpose, including

	programming	system software, application software, and games

Advantages and Applications of C++

Advantages of C++

1. **Performance and Efficiency**: C++ offers direct access to hardware resources, low-level memory manipulation, and fine control over system resources, making it ideal for high-performance applications.
2. **Object-Oriented Programming (OOP)**: Supports classes, inheritance, polymorphism, and encapsulation, allowing developers to create modular, reusable, and scalable code structures.
3. **Extensibility**: C++ allows for the creation of new data types and operators, providing high customization for specific applications.
4. **Standard Template Library (STL)**: STL provides pre-defined classes and functions for data structures and algorithms, which can save time and improve code reliability.
5. **Memory Management**: Offers both automatic and manual memory

management, providing control over memory usage for optimized performance.

6. **Compatibility with C**: C++ is compatible with C code, allowing developers to integrate C libraries and legacy code into C++ applications easily.

7. **Cross-Platform Support**: C++ code can be compiled on different operating systems, which makes it highly portable and adaptable across platforms.

Applications of C++

1. **System Software**: C++ is used in developing operating systems, compilers, and interpreters due to its speed and efficiency. Examples include parts of Windows and Linux operating systems.

2. **Game Development**: C++'s performance is critical in game engines where speed is essential for handling graphics, physics, and real-time processing. Popular game engines like Unreal Engine are built with C++.

3. **Embedded Systems**: The language is often used in embedded systems development, where low-level memory access and real-time execution are necessary.

4. **Real-Time Systems**: C++ is ideal for applications that require real-time responses, such as financial trading

systems, telecommunications, and robotic systems.

5. **GUI Applications**: C++ is widely used for developing graphical user interfaces, including tools like Adobe Photoshop, Illustrator, and GUI libraries like Qt.

6. **Enterprise Software**: Large-scale applications in sectors like finance, banking, and retail benefit from the scalability and performance of C++.

7. **Web Browsers and Database Management Systems**: Browsers (like Firefox) and database engines (like MySQL) are developed in C++ due to its performance and efficiency in handling data-intensive tasks.

Setting Up a C++ Environment

Installing C++ Compilers (GCC, Visual Studio, etc.)

To start coding in C++, you need a compiler that translates your code into machine-readable instructions. Here are common compilers for different operating systems:

- **GCC (GNU Compiler Collection)**: Primarily used on Linux, but also available on Windows via MinGW or WSL

(Windows Subsystem for Linux). To install GCC:

- o **Linux**: Install using package managers, e.g., sudo apt-get install g++ for Ubuntu.
- o **Windows**: Use MinGW (Minimalist GNU for Windows) or WSL to enable Linux environments on Windows.
- o **MacOS**: Install Xcode Command Line Tools by running xcode-select --install in the terminal.
- **Microsoft Visual Studio**: Available on Windows and includes a powerful C++ development environment.
  - o Download and install from the Visual Studio website.
  - o Choose the "Desktop Development with C++" workload to ensure C++ support.
- **Clang**: A compiler from the LLVM project, often used on MacOS and supported on other platforms.
  - o **MacOS**: Pre-installed with Xcode.
  - o **Linux**: Install via package manager, e.g., sudo apt-get install clang.
  - o **Windows**: Available via Visual Studio and can also be installed independently.

Writing and Compiling Your First Program

1. Open a code editor, such as Visual Studio Code, Visual Studio, or even a simple text editor.
2. Write a simple "Hello, World!" program:

```
#include <iostream>

int main() {
    std::cout << "Hello, World!" << std::endl;
    return 0;
}
```

3. Save the file with a . extension (e.g., hello.).
4. Compile the program:
   - **GCC**: Run g++ hello. -o hello in the terminal. This command compiles hello. and outputs an executable named hello.
   - **Visual Studio**: Use the built-in compiler with the "Build" option.
   - **Clang**: Use clang++ hello. -o hello in the terminal.
5. Run the executable:
   - In the terminal, type ./hello (on Linux or MacOS) or hello.exe (on Windows).

Understanding the Structure of a C++ Program

A basic C++ program consists of the following parts:

- **Headers and Libraries**: #include <iostream> imports the standard input-output stream library, enabling the use of std::cout.
- **main() Function**: The main() function is the entry point. Its return type is int, indicating it returns an integer value (typically 0 to indicate success).
- **Statements**: std::cout << "Hello, World!" << std::endl; outputs text to the console. std::endl moves the cursor to a new line.
- **Return Statement**: return 0; indicates that the program ended successfully.

Basic Syntax and Data Types

Basic Syntax (Keywords, Identifiers, Comments)

- **Keywords**: Reserved words like int, return, for, and if have predefined meanings and cannot be used as identifiers.
- **Identifiers**: Names given to variables, functions, and classes, consisting of letters, digits, or underscores (e.g., myVariable).
- **Comments**: Used to document code and ignored by the compiler.

- Single-line comments: // This is a comment
- Multi-line comments: /* This is a multi-line comment */

Data Types: Primitive (int, float, char, etc.) and Derived (arrays, pointers)

- **Primitive Data Types**:
  - int: Integer values, e.g., int a = 5;
  - float and double: Floating-point numbers, e.g., float f = 5.12;
  - char: Single characters, e.g., char c = 'A';
  - bool: Boolean values (true or false).
- **Derived Data Types**:
  - **Arrays**: A collection of elements of the same type, e.g., int arr[5] = {1, 2, 3, 4, 5};
  - **Pointers**: Variables that store memory addresses, e.g., int *ptr = &a;

Variable Declaration and Initialization

Variables should be declared with a type and optionally initialized.

- Declaration: int num;
- Initialization: int num = 10;

Constants and const Keyword

Constants are fixed values that cannot be changed once initialized.

- **Literal Constants**: Directly in the code, like 3.14.
- **Symbolic Constants**: Defined using const, e.g., const int MAX_SIZE = 100;

Operators and Expressions

Arithmetic, Relational, Logical, Bitwise, and Assignment Operators

- **Arithmetic Operators**: +, -, *, /, % (modulus).
  - int result = 10 + 5; // Addition
- **Relational Operators**: Compare values (==, !=, <, >, <=, >=).
- **Logical Operators**: && (AND), | | (OR), ! (NOT).
- **Bitwise Operators**: Perform bit-level operations (&, |, ^, ~, <<, >>).
- **Assignment Operators**: Assign values with =, and compound assignments like +=, -=, *=, etc.

Increment and Decrement Operators

- **Increment**: ++ increases value by 1, e.g., a++ (post-increment) or ++a (pre-increment).
- **Decrement**: -- decreases value by 1, e.g., b-- or --b.

Operator Precedence and Associativity

Operators have a hierarchy of precedence. For example, multiplication has higher precedence than addition:

- **Precedence**: * > + > =
- **Associativity**: Determines the direction in which operators are evaluated. Most binary operators are left-associative, while assignment is right-associative.

Control Flow Statements

Decision-Making: if, else, switch

- **if**: Executes a block of code if a condition is true.

```
if (x > 0) {
    std::cout << "Positive";
}
```

- **else**: Follows an if statement to execute code if the condition is false.

```
if (x > 0) {
    std::cout << "Positive";
} else {
    std::cout << "Non-positive";
}
```

- **else if**: Chains multiple conditions.

```
if (x > 0) {
    std::cout << "Positive";
} else if (x < 0) {
    std::cout << "Negative";
} else {
    std::cout << "Zero";
}
```

- **switch**: Used for selection based on the value of an integer or character.

```
switch (choice) {
    case 1: std::cout << "Option 1"; break;
    case 2: std::cout << "Option 2"; break;
    default: std::cout << "Invalid Option";
}
```

Loops: *for, while, do-while*

- **for**: Used for iteration with initialization, condition, and increment.

```cpp
for (int i = 0; i < 5; i++) {
    std::cout << i;
}
```

- **while**: Loops while a condition is true.

```cpp
int i = 0;
while (i < 5) {
    std::cout << i;
    i++;
}
```

- **do-while**: Similar to while, but checks the condition after executing the loop body at least once.

```cpp
int i = 0;
do {
    std::cout << i;
    i++;
} while (i < 5);
```

Jump Statements: break, continue, goto

- **break**: Exits a loop or switch statement immediately.

```cpp
for (int i = 0; i < 5; i++) {
    if (i == 3) break;
    std::cout << i;
}
```

- **continue**: Skips the current iteration and proceeds to the next iteration.

```cpp
for (int i = 0; i < 5; i++) {
    if (i == 2) continue;
    std::cout << i;
}
```

- **goto**: Transfers control to a labeled statement within the same function (generally discouraged due to readability issues).

```cpp
int i = 0;
begin:
if (i < 5) {
    std::cout << i;
    i++;
    goto begin;
```

}

Functions in C++

Function Declaration, Definition, and Calling

- **Function Declaration (Prototype)**: A
  function declaration specifies the function's
  name, return type, and parameters, but
  does not include the function's body. It
  allows the compiler to check the function
  call before its definition is encountered.

  int add(int, int); // function declaration

- **Function Definition**: The function
  definition provides the actual
  implementation of the function.

  ```
  int add(int a, int b) {
      return a + b;
  }
  ```

- **Function Calling**: A function is called by
  using its name, passing any required
  arguments, and receiving its return value
  (if any).

  int result = add(5, 3); // function call

Scope of Variables (Local, Global, Static)

- **Local Variables**: These are declared inside a function and can only be accessed within that function.

```
void func() {
    int x = 10; // local variable
}
```

- **Global Variables**: These are declared outside any function, and they can be accessed by any function in the program.

```
int globalVar = 5; // global variable
void func() {
    cout << globalVar;
}
```

- **Static Variables**: A variable declared as static retains its value across function calls and does not get reinitialized.

```
void counter() {
    static int count = 0;
    count++;
    cout << count;
}
```

Inline Functions

- Inline functions are small functions that are expanded in place, rather than being called. It improves performance by avoiding the overhead of a function call.

```
inline int square(int x) {
    return x * x;
}
```

Function Overloading

- Function overloading allows multiple functions with the same name but different parameters (either in number or type).

```
int add(int a, int b) { return a + b; }
double add(double a, double b) { return a + b; }
```

Default Arguments and Recursion

- **Default Arguments**: Default values can be provided for parameters in a function definition. If no argument is passed for that parameter, the default value is used.

```
int multiply(int a, int b = 2) {
    return a * b;
}
```

- **Recursion**: A function that calls itself is known as recursion. It is commonly used in problems like factorial calculation, Fibonacci series, etc.

```
int factorial(int n) {
    if (n == 0) return 1;
    return n * factorial(n - 1);
}
```

Pointers and Memory Management

Introduction to Pointers

- A pointer is a variable that stores the memory address of another variable.

```
int a = 10;
int *ptr = &a; // ptr points to a
```

- **Dereferencing**: Access the value stored at the address the pointer is pointing to.

```
cout << *ptr; // prints the value of a
```

Pointer Arithmetic

- Pointers can be incremented or decremented to point to the next or previous memory location.

```
int arr[] = {1, 2, 3};
```

```cpp
int *ptr = arr;
cout << *(ptr + 1); // Accesses arr[1] (prints
2)
```

*Dynamic Memory Allocation: **new** and **delete***

- **new**: Allocates memory dynamically from the heap for a single variable or an array.

```cpp
int *ptr = new int; // Allocates memory for
a single integer
*ptr = 20;
delete ptr; // Frees the memory
```

- **new[] and delete[]**: Used to allocate and deallocate memory for arrays.

```cpp
int *arr = new int[5]; // Allocates memory
for an array of 5 integers
delete[] arr; // Frees the array memory
```

Smart Pointers (from C++11)

- **unique_ptr**: A smart pointer that owns a dynamically allocated object and ensures that the object is automatically destroyed when the pointer goes out of scope.

```cpp
unique_ptr<int> ptr =
make_unique<int>(10);
```

- **shared_ptr**: A smart pointer that maintains a reference count. The object is destroyed when the last shared_ptr to it is destroyed.

  shared_ptr<int> ptr1 = make_shared<int>(20);

- **weak_ptr**: A smart pointer that does not affect the reference count, often used to prevent cyclic references with shared_ptr.

  weak_ptr<int> weakPtr = ptr1;

Arrays and Strings

Array Declaration and Initialization

- Arrays are used to store multiple values of the same data type.

  int arr[5]; // Declare an integer array of size 5
  arr[0] = 1; // Initialize the first element
  int arr2[] = {1, 2, 3, 4, 5}; // Array initialization

Multi-Dimensional Arrays

- Arrays with more than one dimension. Commonly used for matrices or tables.

```cpp
int matrix[2][3] = {{1, 2, 3}, {4, 5, 6}}; // 2x3
matrix
cout << matrix[1][2]; // Prints 6
```

String Manipulation and C++ string Class

- **C-style Strings**: Arrays of characters ending with a null character ('\0').

```cpp
char str[] = "Hello";
cout << str;
```

- **C++ string Class**: Provides various methods for string manipulation like length(), substr(), append(), etc.

```cpp
string s = "Hello";
cout << s.length(); // Prints 5
s.append(" World");
cout << s; // Prints "Hello World"
```

Structures and Unions

Defining and Accessing Structures

- A structure is a user-defined data type that groups related variables.

```cpp
struct Person {
    string name;
    int age;
};
```

```
Person p1;
p1.name = "John";
p1.age = 25;
```

Nested Structures

- Structures can contain other structures as members.

```
struct Address {
    string city;
    string state;
};
struct Person {
    string name;
    Address address;
};
```

Unions and Differences from Structures

- **Union**: A union is similar to a structure but only one member can hold a value at a time. All members share the same memory location.

```
union Data {
    int i;
    float f;
    char c;
};
Data d;
d.i = 5;
```

d.f = 3.14; // Now d.i is overwritten

Enumerations (Enums)

- **Enumerations** allow you to define a variable that can have a set of predefined constants.

  enum Week {Sunday, Monday, Tuesday, Wednesday, Thursday, Friday, Saturday};
  Week today = Monday;

File Handling Basics

File Streams and Classes (ifstream, ofstream, fstream)

- **ifstream**: Used for reading files.

  ifstream file("example.txt");

- **ofstream**: Used for writing to files.

  ofstream file("example.txt");

- **fstream**: Used for both reading and writing.

  fstream file("example.txt", ios::in | ios::out);

Reading and Writing Files

- **Reading from a file**:

```cpp
ifstream file("example.txt");
string line;
while (getline(file, line)) {
    cout << line << endl;
}
```

- **Writing to a file**:

```cpp
ofstream file("example.txt");
file << "Hello, world!" << endl;
```

Basic File Operations (open, close, read, write)

- **open**: Opens a file for reading or writing.

```cpp
ifstream file;
file.open("file.txt");
```

- **close**: Closes the file after operations are complete.

```cpp
file.close();
```

- **read**: Reads from a file into a buffer.

```cpp
char buffer[100];
file.read(buffer, 100);
```

- **write**: Writes data to a file.

```cpp
file.write("Hello", 5);
```

Object-Oriented Programming (OOP) in C++

Introduction to Object-Oriented Programming (OOP)

Basics of OOP: Objects and Classes

- **Object-Oriented Programming (OOP)** is a programming paradigm based on the concept of "objects." These objects represent real-world entities and contain both **data** and **functions** that operate on the data. OOP emphasizes the reusability and organization of code.
  - **Class**: A class is a blueprint or template for creating objects. It defines a data structure and the methods (functions) that can manipulate the data. A class encapsulates data for the object and provides methods to interact with the data.

    class Car {
    public:
        string make;
        string model;
        int year;

```
void start() {
    cout << "Starting the car!" <<
endl;
    }
};
```

- o **Object**: An object is an instance of a class. It holds actual values for the attributes defined in the class and can invoke the class's methods.

```
Car myCar;  // Creating an object of
the class Car
myCar.make = "Toyota";
myCar.model = "Camry";
myCar.year = 2023;
myCar.start();  // Calling the start
method
```

Four Pillars of OOP: Encapsulation, Inheritance, Polymorphism, and Abstraction

- • **Encapsulation**:
  - o Encapsulation refers to bundling the data (variables) and methods (functions) that operate on the data into a single unit called a **class**. It also helps restrict access to certain components using **access specifiers** (public, private, protected).

- Example: A class with private data members, and public getter and setter methods to access them.

```
class Employee {
private:
    string name;
    int age;
public:
    void setName(string n) {
        name = n;
    }
    string getName() {
        return name;
    }
};
```

- **Inheritance**:
  - Inheritance is the mechanism by which one class (derived class) can inherit attributes and methods from another class (base class). It allows the reuse of code and the creation of a hierarchy of classes.
  - Example: The Car class can inherit from a base class Vehicle.

```
class Vehicle {
public:
    int speed;
    void move() {
```

```
    cout << "Moving at speed " <<
speed << " km/h" << endl;
  }
};

class Car : public Vehicle {
public:
  string model;
};
```

- **Polymorphism**:
  - Polymorphism allows one function or method to have multiple forms. It enables the same interface to be used for different data types, making the system flexible and extensible.
  - There are two types of polymorphism:
    - **Compile-time Polymorphism**: Achieved through function overloading and operator overloading.
    - **Run-time Polymorphism**: Achieved using **virtual functions** and method overriding.

```
class Animal {
public:
  virtual void sound() {
```

```cpp
        cout << "Animal sound" <<
endl;
    }
};

class Dog : public Animal {
public:
    void sound() override {
        cout << "Bark" << endl;
    }
};

Animal *a = new Dog();
a->sound(); // Outputs "Bark"
because of polymorphism
```

- **Abstraction**:
  - Abstraction is the process of hiding complex implementation details and showing only the necessary features. This is typically done using **abstract classes** and **interfaces**.
  - An **abstract class** has at least one pure virtual function, which makes it impossible to instantiate directly.

```cpp
class Shape {
public:
```

```cpp
    virtual void draw() = 0; // Pure
virtual function
};

class Circle : public Shape {
public:
    void draw() override {
        cout << "Drawing Circle" <<
endl;
    }
};
```

Classes and Objects

Defining a Class and Creating Objects

- A **class** is defined using the class keyword, followed by the class name, and a set of curly braces containing data members and member functions. A **constructor** is a special method used to initialize objects.

```cpp
class Car {
public:
    string make;
    string model;
    int year;

    // Constructor
    Car(string m, string mo, int y) {
        make = m;
        model = mo;
```

```cpp
        year = y;
    }

    void displayDetails() {
        cout << "Make: " << make << ", Model:
    " << model << ", Year: " << year << endl;
    }
};

// Creating an object and using the
constructor
Car car1("Toyota", "Corolla", 2020);
car1.displayDetails();
```

Access Specifiers: public, private, protected

- **Public**: Members declared as public are accessible from anywhere outside the class. These members are typically functions that provide an interface to the outside world.

```cpp
class Employee {
public:
    string name;
    void setName(string n) {
        name = n;
    }
};
```

- **Private**: Members declared as private are accessible only within the class itself. They

cannot be accessed directly from outside
the class, providing data encapsulation and
security.

```
class Employee {
private:
   string name;
public:
   void setName(string n) {
     name = n;
   }
   string getName() {
     return name;
   }
};
```

- **Protected**: Members declared as protected
  are similar to private but can be accessed by
  derived classes. It is commonly used in
  inheritance to allow derived classes to
  access the base class members while
  keeping them hidden from the outside
  world.

```
class Base {
protected:
   int protectedVar;
};

class Derived : public Base {
public:
```

```
void accessProtectedVar() {
    protectedVar = 10; // Can access
protected member of base class
  }
};
```

Constructors and Destructors

- **Constructor**: A constructor is a special class member function that is automatically called when an object is created. Its primary purpose is to initialize objects.
  - **Types**:
    - **Default Constructor**: A constructor with no parameters.
    - **Parameterized Constructor**: A constructor that takes arguments to initialize object attributes.
    - **Copy Constructor**: A constructor that creates a new object as a copy of an existing object.

```
class Point {
private:
    int x, y;
public:
    // Parameterized constructor
    Point(int a, int b) : x(a), y(b) {}
```

```cpp
    // Default constructor
    Point() : x(0), y(0) {}

    void display() {
        cout << "x: " << x << ", y: " << y
    << endl;
      }
    };
```

- **Destructor**: A destructor is a special member function that is called when an object is destroyed. Its primary purpose is to release any dynamically allocated memory or resources. A destructor does not take parameters and cannot be overloaded.

```cpp
class MyClass {
public:
    MyClass() {
        cout << "Constructor called!" << endl;
    }

    ~MyClass() {
        cout << "Destructor called!" << endl;
    }
};
```

this Pointer

- The this pointer is an implicit pointer that points to the current object. It is automatically passed to all non-static member functions.
- It is used to refer to the current object's data members and functions within the class.

```
class Rectangle {
private:
    int width, height;
public:
    void setDimensions(int width, int height)
    {
        this->width = width;      // Using 'this'
pointer to distinguish between parameter
and member
        this->height = height;
    }

    void display() {
        cout << "Width: " << this->width << ",
Height: " << this->height << endl;
    }
};
```

Encapsulation

Concept of Encapsulation and Data Hiding

- **Encapsulation** is one of the four fundamental principles of Object-Oriented Programming (OOP). It refers to the bundling of data (variables) and methods (functions) that operate on that data into a single unit known as a **class**.
- The primary purpose of encapsulation is to **hide the internal state** of an object from the outside world, exposing only a controlled interface to interact with that data. This process is called **data hiding**.

Key Points:

- o **Data Hiding:** Internal details or state of the object are hidden from the outside world, thus preventing direct access and modification by external code.
- o **Public Interface:** External entities interact with the class through its public methods, also known as the getter and setter methods. These methods ensure that the object's state is modified or accessed in a controlled manner.

Example of Encapsulation:

```
class Car {
private:
    int speed;  // private variable, not
accessible outside

public:
    // Getter function
    int getSpeed() {
        return speed;
    }

    // Setter function
    void setSpeed(int s) {
        if (s >= 0)  // Validating input to
prevent negative speed
            speed = s;
        else
            cout << "Speed cannot be negative!"
<< endl;
    }
};
```

Using Getters and Setters

- **Getters** are public member functions that allow external code to access private data members of a class. They simply "get" the value of the private member.
- **Setters** are public member functions that allow modification of private data members. They are usually used to validate

and control the values being assigned to these private members.

Why Use Getters and Setters?

- **Encapsulation:** They provide a way to encapsulate the internal data of a class.
- **Control:** Setters allow validation of input values, and getters provide a way to safely retrieve the state without direct access to the member variables.
- **Maintenance and Flexibility:** If the internal data representation needs to change, you only need to modify the getter or setter methods without changing external code that uses the class.

Example:

```
class Account {
private:
    double balance;  // Private data member

public:
    // Getter
    double getBalance() {
        return balance;
    }
```

```cpp
// Setter
void setBalance(double amount) {
    if (amount > 0)
        balance = amount;
    else
        cout << "Balance must be positive!" <<
endl;
}
};
```

Benefits of Encapsulation in Real-World Applications

- **Data Integrity and Security:** By restricting direct access to the class's internal data, you ensure that the data cannot be tampered with or corrupted from the outside, preserving the integrity of the object.
- **Modularity:** Encapsulation helps in breaking a large, complex program into smaller, more manageable components, improving maintainability.
- **Code Reusability and Flexibility:** Once encapsulated, the class can be reused in different contexts without worrying about how its internal state is managed. If internal changes are required, the interface remains the same.
- **Reduced Complexity:** Hiding unnecessary implementation details from the user keeps the interface simple and easy to use.

- **Encouraging Best Practices:** By using setters and getters, you enforce good coding practices, such as data validation and separation of concerns.

Inheritance

Introduction to Inheritance and Its Benefits

- **Inheritance** is the mechanism in C++ where one class (the **derived class**) can inherit properties and behaviors (data members and methods) from another class (the **base class**).
- The **derived class** inherits all the public and protected members of the base class, making it easier to create a new class by building upon an existing one.

Benefits of Inheritance:

- **Code Reusability:** Inheritance allows derived classes to reuse the code of the base class, thus minimizing redundancy.
- **Modularity:** New functionality can be added without modifying the existing base class, making it easier to extend the program.
- **Improved Maintainability:** Changes to shared functionality only need to be made in the base class, which propagates to all

derived classes, thus reducing the maintenance overhead.

Example:

```cpp
class Animal {
public:
  void eat() {
    cout << "This animal eats food." << endl;
  }
};

class Dog : public Animal {
public:
  void bark() {
    cout << "The dog barks." << endl;
  }
};
```

Types of Inheritance:

1. **Single Inheritance:** One class derives from one base class.

   class Dog : public Animal { ... };

2. **Multiple Inheritance:** A class can inherit from more than one base class.

   class FlyingAnimal : public Bird, public Bat { ... };

3. **Multilevel Inheritance:** A class derives from another derived class.

    class Mammal : public Animal { ... };
    class Dog : public Mammal { ... };

4. **Hierarchical Inheritance:** Multiple classes derive from a single base class.

    class Dog : public Animal { ... };
    class Cat : public Animal { ... };

5. **Hybrid Inheritance:** A combination of two or more types of inheritance.

    class FlyingMammal : public Mammal, public Bird { ... };

protected Access Specifier

- The **protected** access specifier allows a class's members to be accessible to derived classes but not to external classes.
- It is useful when you want to allow derived classes to inherit or modify the base class's members, but you don't want them to be directly accessible from outside the class.

Example:

class Base {
protected:

```cpp
    int protectedVar;

public:
    Base() : protectedVar(5) {}
};

class Derived : public Base {
public:
    void display() {
        cout << "Accessing protected variable: " <<
protectedVar << endl; // Allowed
    }
};
```

Overriding Base Class Methods

- **Method overriding** occurs when a derived class provides a **new implementation** for a method that is already defined in the base class. The method in the base class should be declared as virtual to support runtime polymorphism.

Example:

```cpp
class Animal {
public:
    virtual void sound() {
        cout << "Animal makes a sound" << endl;
    }
};
```

```cpp
class Dog : public Animal {
public:
  void sound() override {
    cout << "Dog barks" << endl;
  }
};
```

- The **override** keyword ensures that you are correctly overriding a method and helps in preventing errors if the method signature in the base class changes.

Virtual Inheritance to Prevent the Diamond Problem

- **Virtual inheritance** is used in C++ to solve the **diamond problem**, a situation that arises in **multiple inheritance**. The diamond problem occurs when two or more classes inherit from a common base class, leading to ambiguity and duplication of the base class's data members and methods.

Example:

```cpp
class A {
public:
  void display() {
    cout << "Class A" << endl;
  }
```

```
};
```

```
class B : virtual public A {};
class C : virtual public A {};
```

```
class D : public B, public C {};
```

- In this example, **A** is inherited virtually by both **B** and **C**, ensuring that **D** only gets one instance of **A**, avoiding ambiguity.

Key Points of Virtual Inheritance:

- Virtual inheritance ensures that only one instance of the base class is inherited, no matter how many times it appears in the inheritance hierarchy.
- This is achieved by making the inheritance **virtual** when deriving from the base class.

These concepts of **Encapsulation** and **Inheritance** are foundational in C++ and form the core of writing robust, maintainable, and reusable object-oriented code. Each topic provides a stepping stone for advanced concepts and better problem-solving techniques in C++ programming.

Polymorphism in C++

Concept of Polymorphism and Its Types:

Polymorphism is one of the four fundamental principles of Object-Oriented Programming (OOP), and it allows objects of different classes to be treated as objects of a common base class. The word "polymorphism" is derived from the Greek words "poly" (meaning many) and "morph" (meaning forms), which signifies the ability to take on many forms.

Polymorphism is broadly categorized into two types in C++:

1. **Compile-Time Polymorphism (Static Polymorphism):** This type of polymorphism is resolved during the compilation phase. The method or function to be called is determined at compile time. It includes:
   - **Function Overloading**
   - **Operator Overloading**
2. **Runtime Polymorphism (Dynamic Polymorphism):** This type of polymorphism is resolved at runtime, and the function to be executed is determined during program execution. It involves:
   - **Virtual Functions**
   - **Method Overriding**

Compile-Time Polymorphism

Function Overloading:

Function overloading allows multiple functions with the same name but different parameter types or number of parameters. The compiler differentiates between the functions based on their signatures (parameters), and the appropriate function is called based on the argument passed.

```cpp
#include<iostream>
using namespace std;

class Print {
public:
    void show(int i) {
        cout << "Integer: " << i << endl;
    }
    void show(double d) {
        cout << "Double: " << d << endl;
    }
};

int main() {
    Print p;
    p.show(10);     // Calls show(int)
    p.show(10.5);   // Calls show(double)
    return 0;
}
```

Operator Overloading:

Operator overloading allows you to redefine the behavior of operators for user-defined types. For instance, you can define how the addition (+) operator works with objects of a class.

```cpp
#include<iostream>
using namespace std;

class Complex {
private:
    int real, imag;
public:
    Complex() : real(0), imag(0) {}
    Complex(int r, int i) : real(r), imag(i) {}

    // Overloading '+' operator
    Complex operator+(const Complex& c) {
        return Complex(real + c.real, imag + c.imag);
    }

    void display() {
        cout << "Real: " << real << ", Imaginary: " << imag << endl;
    }
};

int main() {
    Complex c1(2, 3), c2(4, 5);
```

```cpp
Complex c3 = c1 + c2; // Calls overloaded '+'
operator
   c3.display();
   return 0;
}
```

Runtime Polymorphism

Virtual Functions:

Virtual functions allow methods in a base class to be overridden in derived classes. The decision about which method to invoke is made at runtime, allowing for dynamic method binding. A virtual function is defined in the base class and is typically overridden in the derived class.

```cpp
#include<iostream>
using namespace std;

class Base {
public:
   virtual void show() { // Virtual function
      cout << "Base Class" << endl;
   }
};

class Derived : public Base {
public:
   void show() override { // Overriding the base
class function
      cout << "Derived Class" << endl;
```

```
    }
};

int main() {
    Base* basePtr;
    Derived derivedObj;

    basePtr = &derivedObj;
    basePtr->show(); // Calls Derived class's show
function
    return 0;
}
```

Method Overriding:

In C++, method overriding is a feature where a
method in a derived class has the same name and
function signature as in the base class but
provides a new implementation. Overriding
requires the base class method to be declared as
virtual.

Abstract Classes and Pure Virtual Functions

Abstract Class:

An abstract class is a class that cannot be
instantiated on its own and is used as a blueprint
for derived classes. It contains at least one **pure
virtual function**. An abstract class may or may not

implement the functions, but it requires derived classes to implement these functions.

```cpp
class AbstractClass {
public:
    virtual void show() = 0; // Pure virtual function
};
```

Pure Virtual Function:

A pure virtual function is a function that has no definition in the base class, forcing the derived classes to provide an implementation. It is denoted by assigning = 0 to the function declaration.

```cpp
#include<iostream>
using namespace std;

class Shape {
public:
    virtual void draw() = 0; // Pure virtual function
};

class Circle : public Shape {
public:
    void draw() override {
        cout << "Drawing Circle" << endl;
    }
```

```cpp
};

int main() {
    // Shape s;  // Error: cannot instantiate abstract class
    Circle c;
    c.draw();
    return 0;
}
```

Abstraction in C++

Concept of Abstraction and Its Benefits:

Abstraction is the principle of hiding the internal workings of a system and exposing only the essential features to the outside world. It allows a programmer to focus on high-level functionality while ignoring unnecessary implementation details. Abstraction is closely related to information hiding.

- **Benefits of Abstraction:**
  - **Simplified Interface:** It provides a simplified view of the system, reducing complexity.
  - **Improved Maintainability:** Changes to the internal implementation do not affect the external interface.

- Increased Security: It hides implementation details that are not necessary for the user to know.

In C++, abstraction is implemented through:

- **Abstract Classes**
- **Pure Virtual Functions**

Abstract Classes vs. Interfaces (in C++)

- **Abstract Class:**
  - Can have both abstract (pure virtual) and concrete (implemented) methods.
  - May have member variables.
  - Derived classes can inherit and override virtual functions.
  - Supports multiple inheritance.
- **Interface:**
  - In C++, the concept of an interface is simulated using an abstract class with only pure virtual functions.
  - Contains no data members and only pure virtual methods.
  - Cannot have any implemented methods or member variables.

Difference:

- **Abstract Classes** allow both pure virtual and concrete methods. They may have data members.
- **Interfaces** are used purely to define the contract for the derived class to follow and have no implemented functionality or member variables.

```
class Interface {
public:
   virtual void func() = 0; // Pure virtual function
};


class AbstractClass {
public:
   virtual void func() = 0; // Pure virtual function
   void concreteMethod() {
     // Some implementation
   }
};
```

Real-World Examples of Abstraction in C++

1. **Vehicle Example (Using Abstract Classes):** Consider a real-world scenario where you want to represent different types of vehicles like Car, Truck, and Bicycle. Each of these types of vehicles has some common operations (e.g., start(), stop()), but the implementation will vary. An abstract class can represent the general concept of a

Vehicle, and the derived classes will implement the specific details.

```cpp
class Vehicle {
public:
    virtual void start() = 0; // Abstract method
    virtual void stop() = 0;  // Abstract method
};

class Car : public Vehicle {
public:
    void start() override {
        cout << "Car starting" << endl;
    }
    void stop() override {
        cout << "Car stopping" << endl;
    }
};

class Truck : public Vehicle {
public:
    void start() override {
        cout << "Truck starting" << endl;
    }
    void stop() override {
        cout << "Truck stopping" << endl;
    }
};
```

2. **Bank Account Example (Using Abstraction for Security):** A BankAccount class may have operations like deposit() and withdraw(). You can abstract away details such as how the account balance is maintained and instead expose only the necessary methods, allowing users to interact with the account without knowing the underlying implementation.

```
class BankAccount {
private:
    double balance; // Data hidden from
outside world
public:
    void deposit(double amount) {
        balance += amount;
    }
    void withdraw(double amount) {
        if (balance >= amount) {
            balance -= amount;
        }
    }
    double getBalance() {
        return balance;
    }
};
```

In these examples, abstraction helps encapsulate complex behavior and provides clear interfaces for interacting with objects.

11. Operator Overloading in C++

Basics of Operator Overloading

Operator overloading is a feature in C++ that allows you to define custom behavior for operators (such as +, -, *, /, etc.) when they are used with user-defined data types (like classes or structs). Essentially, it allows an operator to act on objects of a class as if they were built-in types.

By overloading operators, you can make your custom objects behave similarly to primitive types, which helps in improving code readability and making it more intuitive.

For example, the + operator, which normally adds two numbers, can be redefined for a class (e.g., Complex numbers) to perform addition between two objects of that class.

Syntax for Overloading an Operator:

```
class ClassName {
public:
    returnType operator symbol (parameter_list) {
        // function body
```

```
    }
};
```

Example of operator overloading for the + operator:

```
class Complex {
private:
    float real;
    float imag;

public:
    Complex(float r, float i) : real(r), imag(i) {}

    // Overloading the + operator
    Complex operator+(const Complex &obj) {
        return Complex(real + obj.real, imag +
obj.imag);
    }

    void display() {
        cout << real << " + " << imag << "i" << endl;
    }
};

int main() {
    Complex num1(3.2, 4.5), num2(1.3, 2.5);
    Complex result = num1 + num2;
    result.display(); // Output: 4.5 + 7.0i
    return 0;
}
```

Overloading Arithmetic, Comparison, and Assignment Operators

1. **Arithmetic Operators (+, -, *, /)**
   o These operators can be overloaded for custom classes to perform arithmetic operations between objects.
   o Example: Overloading the + operator to add two objects of a Complex class (as shown above).
2. **Comparison Operators (==, !=, <, >, <=, >=)**
   o Comparison operators can be overloaded to compare objects of a class based on the values of their data members.
   o Example: Overloading the == operator to compare two Complex numbers.

   ```
   bool operator==(const Complex &obj) {
       return (real == obj.real && imag == obj.imag);
   }
   ```

3. **Assignment Operator (=)**
   o The assignment operator is overloaded to ensure that when one object is assigned to another, a proper deep copy is made,

particularly when dynamic memory allocation is involved.

- o **Syntax**: ClassName& operator=(const ClassName& other).

Example of overloading the assignment operator:

```
class Complex {
private:
    float real, imag;

public:
    Complex(float r, float i) : real(r), imag(i)
{}

    Complex& operator=(const Complex
&obj) {
        if (this != &obj) { // Self-assignment
check
            real = obj.real;
            imag = obj.imag;
        }
        return *this;
    }
};
```

Rules and Restrictions for Operator Overloading

- **Operators That Cannot Be Overloaded**:
    1. :: (Scope resolution operator)

2. . (Member access operator)
3. .* (Pointer-to-member operator)
4. ?: (Ternary conditional operator)
5. sizeof (Size operator)
- **Key Points**:
   1. The overloaded operator must behave according to its original functionality.
   2. It cannot change the number of operands (i.e., binary operators cannot become unary).
   3. The return type should reflect the operation's expected result (e.g., returning an object when overloading arithmetic operators).
   4. Operator overloading is not a "magic trick" — it should improve code clarity, not confuse the reader.

Friend Functions and Friend Classes in C++

Definition and Uses of Friend Functions

A **friend function** in C++ is a function that is not a member of a class but has the privilege to access the class's private and protected members. A friend function can be either a regular function or a method of another class, and it is declared by using the friend keyword inside the class definition.

Syntax for Declaring a Friend Function:

```
class ClassName {
    private:
        int data;

    public:
        friend void friendFunction(ClassName &obj);
// Friend function declaration
};

void friendFunction(ClassName &obj) {
    cout << "Accessing private data: " << obj.data
<< endl;
}
```

In the above example, friendFunction is able to access the private data member of ClassName even though it is not a member function of ClassName.

Friend Classes and Their Applications

A **friend class** is a class whose member functions can access the private and protected members of another class. A class can declare another class as a friend by using the friend keyword, and the second class can access private and protected members of the first class.

Syntax for Declaring a Friend Class:

```cpp
class ClassA {
    private:
        int data;

    public:
        friend class ClassB;  // ClassB is a friend of ClassA
};

class ClassB {
    public:
        void display(ClassA &obj) {
            cout << "Accessing private data of ClassA: " << obj.data << endl;
        }
};
```

In this example, ClassB is a friend of ClassA, so it can access the private member data of ClassA.

Applications:

- Friend functions and classes are useful in situations where one class needs to access the internals of another class but does not make sense to make it a member function.
- They are commonly used in operator overloading (for operators that work between different classes).
- Friend functions are also useful when implementing certain types of relationships

between classes, such as helper or utility classes.

Pros and Cons of Friend Functions

Pros:

1. **Access to Private Data**: Friend functions can access private and protected data members, enabling them to perform specialized operations that require such access.
2. **Improved Encapsulation**: By declaring a function as a friend, a class can control which functions can access its internal data, preserving the concept of encapsulation.
3. **Operator Overloading**: Friend functions are often used for overloading operators that need to operate between two classes.

Cons:

1. **Violation of Encapsulation**: While friend functions are useful, they do violate encapsulation to an extent because they allow external functions to access a class's private data.
2. **Tight Coupling**: Friend functions and classes can introduce tight coupling between classes, making the system less modular and harder to maintain.

3. **Maintenance Issues**: If a class exposes too many private members to external functions, it can become difficult to change the internal implementation without affecting many other parts of the code.

Example of Friend Functions and Classes:

```cpp
#include<iostream>
using namespace std;

class B; // Forward declaration

class A {
private:
    int x;
public:
    A() : x(10) {}
    friend void showA(A &a, B &b); // Friend
function declaration
};

class B {
private:
    int y;
public:
    B() : y(20) {}
    friend void showA(A &a, B &b); // Friend
function declaration
};
```

```cpp
void showA(A &a, B &b) {
    cout << "Accessing A's private x: " << a.x <<
endl;
    cout << "Accessing B's private y: " << b.y <<
endl;
}

int main() {
    A a;
    B b;
    showA(a, b);  // Both classes access each other's
private data
    return 0;
}
```

Output:

Accessing A's private x: 10
Accessing B's private y: 20

In the example, showA is a friend function that
can access private members of both A and B
classes, which shows the power and flexibility of
using friend functions and classes.

11. Templates in C++

Introduction to Templates and Generic Programming

- **Templates** in C++ allow you to write functions and classes that can work with any data type. This enables **generic programming,** where you can write code without specifying the exact types of data you want to work with. Templates enable code reusability, making programs more flexible and adaptable.
- **Why Use Templates?**
  - **Reusability**: One function or class can work with different types of data.
  - **Type Safety**: Templates are statically typed, ensuring compile-time type checking.
  - **Efficiency**: Templates allow for efficient code since the type-specific code is generated during compilation.

Function Templates and Class Templates

1. **Function Templates**
   - A **function template** defines a pattern for functions that can operate on any data type. The compiler generates a specific version

of the function for each type when the function is called.

- Syntax:

```
template <typename T>
T add(T a, T b) {
    return a + b;
}
```

- **typename** or **class** (interchangeable) is a placeholder for any data type.
- When you call add<int>(3, 4), the compiler creates a version of add that works with int.

- **Example**:

```
#include <iostream>
template <typename T>
T multiply(T a, T b) {
    return a * b;
}

int main() {
    std::cout << multiply(3, 4) << std::endl; // Works with integers
    std::cout << multiply(2.5, 3.5) << std::endl; // Works with doubles
    return 0;
}
```

2. **Class Templates**
   - A **class template** works similarly to function templates but is used to define classes or structs that operate on generic types.
   - Syntax:

   ```
   template <typename T>
   class Box {
   private:
       T value;
   public:
       Box(T val) : value(val) {}
       T getValue() { return value; }
   };
   ```

     - You can create objects of different types using the class template, such as Box<int>, Box<double>, etc.
   - **Example**:

   ```
   #include <iostream>
   template <typename T>
   class Container {
   private:
       T value;
   public:
       Container(T val) : value(val) {}
       void display() { std::cout <<
   "Value: " << value << std::endl; }
   ```

```
};

int main() {
    Container<int> intContainer(10);
    intContainer.display();

    Container<std::string>
    stringContainer("Hello");
    stringContainer.display();

    return 0;
}
```

Template Specialization

- **Template specialization** allows you to define a custom implementation for a specific data type when needed. This is helpful when the generic version of the template doesn't work as intended for certain types.

1. **Full Specialization**:
   - You define a specific version of a template for a particular type.

```
template <typename T>
class Printer {
public:
    void print(T value) {
        std::cout << value << std::endl;
```

```cpp
    }
};

// Full specialization for `char*`
template <>
class Printer<char*> {
public:
    void print(char* value) {
        std::cout << "String: " << value << std::endl;
    }
};

int main() {
    Printer<int> intPrinter;
    intPrinter.print(10); // Uses general template

    Printer<char*> charPrinter;
    charPrinter.print("Hello, World!"); // Uses specialized template for char*
    return 0;
}
```

2. **Partial Specialization**:
    - You can specialize a template for a subset of types.


```cpp
template <typename T, typename U>
```

```cpp
class Pair {
private:
    T first;
    U second;
public:
    Pair(T f, U s) : first(f), second(s) {}
    void display() {
        std::cout << first << ", " << second <<
std::endl;
    }
};

// Specialization for when both types are
the same
template <typename T>
class Pair<T, T> {
private:
    T first;
public:
    Pair(T f) : first(f) {}
    void display() {
        std::cout << "Single: " << first <<
std::endl;
    }
};

int main() {
    Pair<int, double> p1(10, 20.5);
    p1.display(); // Uses general template
```

```cpp
    Pair<int, int> p2(10);
    p2.display(); // Uses specialized
template
    return 0;
}
```

Exception Handling in C++

Basics of Exception Handling in C++

- **Exception handling** allows the
  programmer to manage runtime errors by
  transferring control to special functions
  known as **exception handlers**. This
  mechanism improves program stability by
  separating error-handling logic from
  regular code.
- **Why Use Exception Handling?**
  - **Separation of concerns**: Exception
    handling separates error-handling
    code from regular logic.
  - **Error Propagation**: Errors can be
    propagated through multiple
    function calls without cluttering the
    code with error checks.
  - **Clean and maintainable code**:
    Exception handling avoids the need
    for extensive error codes and
    provides a clear flow for handling
    errors.

try, catch, throw Keywords

1. **try Block**: This block contains code that might throw an exception. If an exception occurs, control is transferred to the corresponding catch block.

```
try {
    // Code that might throw an exception
}
```

2. **throw Keyword**: Used to explicitly throw an exception when an error occurs. The throw keyword can be used to throw any type of object (including primitive types, class objects, or user-defined types).

```
throw exceptionType;
```

3. **catch Block**: Catches exceptions thrown from the try block. The type of exception it catches is specified inside the parentheses.

```
try {
    throw 10;  // Throwing an integer exception
}
catch (int e) {
    std::cout << "Caught exception: " << e << std::endl;
}
```

o **Example**:

```
#include <iostream>
class MyException {};

int main() {
    try {
        throw MyException();
    }
    catch (MyException& e) {
        std::cout << "Caught a MyException!" << std::endl;
    }
    return 0;
}
```

Standard Exception Classes

- The **Standard Library** in C++ provides several predefined exception classes that can be used for error handling. These include:
  - o std::exception: The base class for all standard exceptions.
  - o std::runtime_error: For errors that occur during program execution.
  - o std::invalid_argument: For invalid arguments passed to a function.

- o std::out_of_range: For accessing out-of-bound elements in containers.
- o std::bad_alloc: For memory allocation failures.

Example:

```
#include <iostream>
#include <stdexcept>

int main() {
    try {
        throw std::invalid_argument("Invalid argument exception!");
    }
    catch (const std::invalid_argument& e) {
        std::cout << "Caught: " << e.what() << std::endl;
    }
    return 0;
}
```

Creating Custom Exceptions

- You can create custom exception classes by inheriting from std::exception or any other exception class. This allows you to define your own exception types, each with specific behavior and messages.
- **Syntax for Custom Exception**:

```cpp
class MyException : public std::exception {
public:
    const char* what() const noexcept
override {
        return "This is a custom exception!";
    }
};
```

- **Example**:

```cpp
#include <iostream>
class MyException : public std::exception {
public:
    const char* what() const noexcept
override {
        return "Custom exception occurred!";
    }
};

int main() {
    try {
        throw MyException();
    }
    catch (const MyException& e) {
        std::cout << "Caught exception: " <<
e.what() << std::endl;
    }
    return 0;
}
```

- **what() Method**: The what() method is inherited from std::exception and returns a message explaining the exception. It can be overridden to provide specific messages for custom exceptions.

.

Modern C++ Concepts

21. Lambda Expressions

Basics of Lambda Expressions and Their Syntax

Lambda expressions are anonymous functions that can be defined in place, without the need to explicitly declare a function. They are especially useful for short-lived tasks or in situations where a function is needed temporarily.

Syntax:

[capture_clause] (parameter_list) -> return_type { function_body }

- **Capture Clause**: Specifies how variables from the surrounding scope are captured by the lambda.
- **Parameter List**: Like function parameters, but optional if not needed.
- **Return Type**: Optional. If omitted, it is inferred by the compiler.
- **Function Body**: The block where the lambda logic is defined.

Example:

auto add = [](int a, int b) -> int { return a + b; };
std::cout << add(3, 4); // Output: 7

Capturing Variables by Value and Reference

Lambda expressions can capture variables from the surrounding scope, either by value or by reference.

- **By Value**: The captured variables are copied into the lambda. Changes made inside the lambda do not affect the original variables.

  ```
  int x = 10;
  auto capture_by_value = [x]() { return x * 2;
  };
  x = 20;
  std::cout << capture_by_value(); //
  Output: 20 (captures initial value)
  ```

- **By Reference**: The lambda captures the variables by reference, allowing the lambda to modify the original variables.

  ```
  int x = 10;
  auto capture_by_reference = [&x]() { x = x *
  2; };
  capture_by_reference();
  std::cout << x; // Output: 20 (modifies the
  original variable)
  ```

- **Capture All by Value or Reference**: You can capture all variables either by value or reference:
  - [=] (Capture all by value)
  - [&] (Capture all by reference)

Practical Use Cases of Lambdas

- **Sorting**: Lambdas can be used as custom comparison functions in sorting algorithms.

  std::vector<int> nums = {3, 1, 4, 1, 5, 9};
  std::sort(nums.begin(), nums.end(), [](int a, int b) { return a < b; });

- **Callbacks**: Lambdas are often used for short callback functions in algorithms like std::for_each.

  std::for_each(nums.begin(), nums.end(), [](int num) { std::cout << num << " "; });

- **Functional Programming**: Lambdas can be used in functional programming paradigms, such as with std::transform to apply a transformation to each element in a collection.

STL (Standard Template Library)

Overview of STL Components: Containers, Iterators, Algorithms

The **Standard Template Library (STL)** is a collection of template classes and functions that provide general-purpose algorithms and data structures.

1. **Containers**: Data structures that store objects, including arrays, linked lists, trees, and hash tables.
2. **Iterators**: Objects that allow traversal of containers in a uniform way.
3. **Algorithms**: Generic algorithms that can operate on containers using iterators (e.g., sorting, searching, etc.).

Common Containers: vector, list, map, set

- **vector**: A dynamic array that grows in size. It provides fast random access and efficient operations at the end (push_back, pop_back).

  std::vector<int> v = {1, 2, 3};
  v.push_back(4);

- **list**: A doubly linked list that allows for efficient insertions and deletions anywhere but slower access to elements compared to vector.

```cpp
std::list<int> l = {1, 2, 3};
l.push_back(4);
```

- **map**: A key-value pair collection, similar to a hash table, where each key is unique, and the value is associated with the key.

```cpp
std::map<std::string, int> age;
age["Alice"] = 25;
age["Bob"] = 30;
```

- **set**: A collection of unique elements, typically used for membership tests.

```cpp
std::set<int> s = {1, 2, 3};
s.insert(4);
```

Using Algorithms like sort, find, for_each

- **sort**: Sorts elements in a container using a comparison function or the default < operator.

```cpp
std::vector<int> nums = {5, 2, 8, 1};
std::sort(nums.begin(), nums.end());
```

- **find**: Searches for a specific value in a container and returns an iterator to it.

```cpp
auto it = std::find(nums.begin(),
nums.end(), 8);
```

- **for_each**: Applies a function to each element in a container.

  std::for_each(nums.begin(), nums.end(), [](int n) { std::cout << n << " "; });

Move Semantics and Rvalue References

Concept of Rvalue and Lvalue References

- **Lvalue**: An object that occupies some identifiable location in memory (e.g., a variable).
- **Rvalue**: A temporary object that does not have a permanent memory address, such as the result of an arithmetic operation.
- **Lvalue Reference**: T& allows modifying the object referred to.

  int x = 5;
  int& ref = x; // ref is an lvalue reference

- **Rvalue Reference**: T&& allows "stealing" the resources from temporary objects.

  int&& temp = 5; // temp is an rvalue reference

std::move and std::forward

- **std::move**: Converts an lvalue to an rvalue, enabling move semantics.

```cpp
std::vector<int> a = {1, 2, 3};
std::vector<int> b = std::move(a); //
Moves resources from a to b
```

- **std::forward**: Used in function templates to perfectly forward arguments while preserving their value category (lvalue or rvalue).

```cpp
template <typename T>
void wrapper(T&& arg) {
    func(std::forward<T>(arg)); // Forward
arg preserving its value category
}
```
Perfect Forwarding

Perfect forwarding ensures that the arguments passed to a function template are forwarded to another function, preserving their value category (lvalue or rvalue).

```cpp
template <typename T>
void func(T&& arg) {
    another_func(std::forward<T>(arg)); //
Perfectly forwards the argument
}
```

Smart Pointers (in Detail)

Types of Smart Pointers: unique_ptr, shared_ptr, weak_ptr

- **unique_ptr**: A smart pointer that owns and manages a resource, ensuring only one unique_ptr can own a given resource at any time.

  std::unique_ptr<int> ptr = std::make_unique<int>(10);

- **shared_ptr**: A smart pointer that allows multiple owners for the same resource. The resource is deallocated when the last shared_ptr is destroyed.

  std::shared_ptr<int> ptr1 = std::make_shared<int>(10); std::shared_ptr<int> ptr2 = ptr1; // Both share ownership

- **weak_ptr**: A smart pointer that doesn't affect the reference count of the object. It's used to prevent circular references in shared ownership scenarios.

  std::weak_ptr<int> weak = ptr1;

Benefits of Using Smart Pointers over Raw Pointers

- Automatic memory management: Smart pointers prevent memory leaks by automatically deallocating memory when the pointer goes out of scope.
- Safer and easier to use compared to raw pointers, especially in complex systems with shared ownership or circular references.

Reference Counting and Object Lifetime Management

- **Reference counting**: Both shared_ptr and weak_ptr use reference counting to track the number of pointers pointing to a resource. When the count reaches zero, the resource is automatically deleted.

Multithreading and Concurrency (Advanced)

Basic Concepts of Multithreading

Multithreading allows a program to execute multiple threads concurrently. Each thread has its execution path, which can run in parallel, improving performance in multi-core processors.

- **Thread**: The basic unit of CPU execution.

- **Concurrency**: The ability to execute multiple tasks concurrently, not necessarily in parallel.

std::thread, std::mutex, std::lock_guard

- **std::thread**: Used to create and manage threads.

```
void thread_func() {
    std::cout << "Hello from thread\n";
}

std::thread t(thread_func);
t.join(); // Wait for thread to finish
```

- **std::mutex**: A mutual exclusion object used to protect shared resources from concurrent access by multiple threads.

```
std::mutex mtx;
mtx.lock();
// Critical section
mtx.unlock();
```

- **std::lock_guard**: A safer way to lock and unlock mutexes using RAII (Resource Acquisition Is Initialization).

```
std::lock_guard<std::mutex> guard(mtx);
```

```
// Mutex is locked here, and unlocked
when guard goes out of scope
```

Introduction to Asynchronous Programming with std::async

std::async is used to run a task asynchronously, returning a std::future that can be used to obtain the result once the task is completed.

```
std::future<int> fut =
std::async(std::launch::async, []() { return 42; });
int result = fut.get(); // Waits for result and
retrieves it
```

4o mini

Practical C++ Tips

Code Optimization Tips

Techniques for Writing Efficient C++ Code
Efficient C++ code is crucial for performance, particularly in applications like game development, real-time systems, or high-performance computing. Code optimization can be approached at different levels: from high-level algorithm design to low-level memory management. Here are some key techniques:

1. **Algorithm Optimization**:
   - **Choose the right data structures**: Use efficient data structures such as hash tables (for fast lookups) or balanced trees (for ordered data). The correct data structure can dramatically reduce the time complexity of operations (e.g., using std::map instead of an unsorted std::vector for searching).
   - **Use algorithms from the Standard Template Library (STL)**: The STL algorithms are highly optimized for performance. Functions like std::sort(), std::find(), and std::transform() are often more

efficient than custom implementations.

2. **Avoiding Unnecessary Computations**:
   - **Precompute Results**: If a computation's result can be stored and reused later, avoid redundant calculations. For example, instead of calculating the same value in a loop, calculate it once before the loop starts.
   - **Loop Unrolling**: This technique involves manually expanding a loop to reduce the overhead of the loop control structure. This can sometimes increase performance, especially when the loop body is small.

3. **Memory Optimization**:
   - **Avoiding Memory Fragmentation**: Fragmented memory can degrade performance over time. Allocating large blocks of memory at once and reusing them instead of allocating and deallocating small chunks can help.
   - **Use Stack Memory Over Heap Memory**: If the object's lifetime is short and it doesn't need to be shared, prefer stack allocation over heap allocation. Stack allocation is

faster and does not involve memory fragmentation.

4. **Inlining Functions**:
   o **Inline Small Functions**: For small, frequently called functions, use the inline keyword. This suggests to the compiler to replace the function call with the function code itself, reducing the overhead of function calls.

5. **Cache Optimization**:
   o **Data Locality**: Accessing elements in memory sequentially is generally faster than accessing them randomly. Organize data structures so that frequently used data is located near each other in memory.
   o **Prefetching**: This involves preloading data into the CPU cache before it's actually needed to reduce cache misses.

6. **Compiler Optimizations**:
   o Use compiler optimization flags (e.g., -O2, -O3 in GCC) to enable various levels of optimization. These optimizations include inlining functions, loop unrolling, and reducing function call overhead.

Using const Correctly, Avoiding Expensive Copy Operations

1. **Using const Correctly**:
   - **const for Read-Only Variables**:
     Using const ensures that a variable cannot be accidentally modified, which improves both the safety and clarity of the code. Example:

     const int x = 10;

   - **const in Function Parameters**:
     Marking function parameters as const allows the compiler to optimize the code and prevents accidental modification of passed arguments.

     void print(const std::string& str);

   - **const Member Functions**: Member functions that do not modify the state of the object should be marked as const to guarantee that no changes occur. This enables better optimization and makes the code clearer.

     ```
     class MyClass {
     public:
         int getValue() const { return value;
     }
     private:
     ```

```
    int value;
};
```

2. **Avoiding Expensive Copy Operations**:
   o **Pass by Reference**: Whenever possible, pass large objects by reference (preferably const reference) instead of by value to avoid unnecessary copies. Example:

   ```
   void processData(const LargeObject& obj);
   ```

   o **Use Move Semantics**: With C++11 and above, use move semantics to avoid expensive copying of objects. Move operations transfer resources from one object to another without copying data. Example:

   ```
   std::vector<int> getLargeVector() {
       std::vector<int> temp = {1, 2, 3, 4, 5};
       return temp; // Move semantic is used here
   }
   ```

Common Mistakes and Debugging Tips

Common C++ Pitfalls

1. **Dangling Pointers**:
   o A dangling pointer occurs when an object is deleted, but a pointer to it still exists. Dereferencing this pointer can cause undefined behavior.
   o **Solution**: Set pointers to nullptr after deleting them:

   delete ptr;
   ptr = nullptr; // Prevents dangling pointer

2. **Memory Leaks**:
   o Memory leaks occur when dynamically allocated memory is not deallocated, leading to resource exhaustion over time.
   o **Solution**: Use smart pointers (std::unique_ptr, std::shared_ptr) to automatically manage memory. If manual memory management is used, ensure that every new operation is paired with a delete operation.

   std::unique_ptr<MyClass> ptr = std::make_unique<MyClass>();

3. **Null Pointer Dereferencing**:

- Dereferencing a nullptr leads to undefined behavior.
- **Solution**: Always check pointers for nullptr before dereferencing:

```
if (ptr != nullptr) {
    // Safe to dereference ptr
}
```

4. **Undefined Behavior with Uninitialized Variables**:
   - Accessing uninitialized variables leads to unpredictable results.
   - **Solution**: Always initialize variables before use:

   ```
   int x = 0; // Initialize variables
   ```

5. **Incorrect Use of == and =**:
   - Using the assignment operator (=) instead of the equality operator (==) in conditionals is a common error.
   - **Solution**: Always check for logical errors between the two operators. Consider using a compiler flag (e.g., -Wall in GCC) to warn about assignments within conditions.

Best Practices for Debugging and Testing

1. **Use of Debugging Tools**:

- gdb (GNU Debugger): GDB allows stepping through code, inspecting variables, and controlling program execution. It helps identify logical and runtime errors.
- Valgrind: Useful for detecting memory leaks and improper memory accesses.
- Sanitizers: Use AddressSanitizer, UndefinedBehaviorSanitizer, and ThreadSanitizer to detect various runtime issues.

2. **Unit Testing:**
   - Write unit tests to ensure that individual components of your program work as expected. Libraries like **Google Test** or **Catch2** can be used for testing.
   - Automate tests as part of a build process to catch bugs early.

3. **Logging:**
   - Use logging mechanisms to track the execution flow, especially for complex or multi-threaded programs. Libraries like **spdlog** or **Boost.Log** can be used for efficient logging.

4. **Code Reviews:**
   - Regular code reviews help spot mistakes, enforce coding standards,

and ensure that best practices are followed.

Important C++ Libraries and Resources

Overview of Useful C++ Libraries

1. **Boost**:
   - **Boost** is one of the most widely used libraries in C++. It provides a wide range of features, including smart pointers, containers, algorithms, threading, and more.
   - Key modules:
     - **Boost.SmartPtr**: Implements advanced smart pointer functionality.
     - **Boost.Thread**: Multi-threading support.
     - **Boost.Asio**: Asynchronous input/output for network programming.
2. **Qt**:
   - **Qt** is a powerful cross-platform library for developing GUI applications, with support for networking, databases, and more.
   - Provides tools for building windows, dialogs, and widgets, and includes features like signals and slots for event handling.

o Qt is highly optimized for performance and supports a variety of platforms, making it a go-to library for desktop applications.

3. **STL (Standard Template Library):**
   o The **STL** is an essential part of C++ and includes commonly used containers (like std::vector, std::list, std::map), algorithms (like std::sort, std::find), and iterators.
   o STL containers are generic and provide high performance.

4. **OpenCV:**
   o **OpenCV** is a library designed for real-time computer vision. It offers a set of functions for image processing, machine learning, and computer vision tasks.

5. **Eigen:**
   o **Eigen** is a high-performance library for linear algebra, matrix operations, and numerical computation. It is widely used in scientific computing and machine learning.

Reliable Resources and Communities for C++ Developers

1. **Official C++ Documentation:**

- The ISO C++ website provides standards, resources, and updates on the language.
- reference.com is a comprehensive reference for C++.

2. **C++ Blogs and Tutorials**:
   - **The C++ Programming Language** (Bjarne Stroustrup's official blog)
   - **Fluent C++**: A blog focused on modern C++ best practices and advanced topics.

3. **Online Communities**:
   - **Stack Overflow**: A huge Q&A community where you can find answers to most C++ questions.
   - **Reddit's r/**: A place for discussions, news, and tutorials related to C++ development.

4. **Books**:
   - **"Effective C++" by Scott Meyers**: A great book for understanding the best practices and subtleties of C++.
   - **"The C++ Programming Language" by Bjarne Stroustrup**: The definitive guide by the creator of C++.

By leveraging these libraries and resources, C++ developers can access powerful tools and stay up-to-date with best practices in the field.

C++ Interview Questions and Answers

1. What is the difference between C++ and C?

Answer: C++ is an extension of C that introduces object-oriented programming (OOP) features such as classes, inheritance, polymorphism, and encapsulation. C is a procedural language focused on functions, while C++ supports both procedural and object-oriented paradigms.

2. What are the advantages of using C++?

Answer:

- Object-Oriented Programming: Supports encapsulation, inheritance, and polymorphism.
- Memory Management: Offers control over memory using pointers.
- High Performance: C++ allows low-level manipulation, which is useful for system-level programming.
- Extensive Standard Library: Includes useful data structures and algorithms.
- Cross-Platform: Supports multiple operating systems.

3. What is a pointer in C++?

Answer: A pointer is a variable that stores the memory address of another variable. Pointers are used for dynamic memory allocation, arrays, and functions. They provide a way to manipulate memory directly, which is useful in system-level programming.

4. Explain the use of new and delete in C++.

Answer: new is used to allocate memory dynamically on the heap, while delete is used to free up that memory. They help in managing memory manually. For example:

```
int* ptr = new int(10); // allocate memory
delete ptr; // deallocate memory
```

5. What is a reference variable in C++?

Answer: A reference is an alias for another variable. Once a reference is initialized to a variable, it cannot be changed to reference another variable. It is used to pass arguments to functions efficiently.

```
int a = 5;
int& ref = a; // reference to a
ref = 10; // a is now 10
```

6. What is the difference between ++i and i++?

Answer: ++i is a pre-increment operator, which increments i before its value is used in an expression. i++ is a post-increment operator, which uses i's current value in the expression and then increments it.

```
int i = 5;
cout << ++i; // outputs 6
cout << i++; // outputs 6, but i becomes 7
```

7. What is a constructor in C++?

Answer: A constructor is a special member function that is automatically called when an object of a class is created. It is used to initialize objects. Constructors can be overloaded.

```
class MyClass {
public:
    MyClass() { // Default constructor
        cout << "Object created!" << endl;
    }
};
```

8. Explain the concept of function overloading in C++.

Answer: Function overloading allows multiple functions to have the same name but different parameter lists. The correct function is called based on the arguments passed.

```cpp
void print(int i) { cout << i; }
void print(double d) { cout << d; }
```

9. What is inheritance in C++?

Answer: Inheritance is a feature in C++ that allows a class (derived class) to inherit properties and behaviors (methods) from another class (base class). This promotes code reuse and establishes a hierarchy.

```cpp
class Animal {
public:
   void speak() { cout << "Animal speaks"; }
};

class Dog : public Animal {
public:
   void bark() { cout << "Dog barks"; }
};
```

10. What is polymorphism in C++?

Answer: Polymorphism allows functions or methods to behave differently based on the object type. There are two types:

- Compile-time polymorphism (function overloading, operator overloading)
- Runtime polymorphism (achieved through virtual functions and inheritance)

11. What is the difference between public, private, and protected access specifiers?

Answer:

- public: Members are accessible from anywhere.
- private: Members are only accessible within the class.
- protected: Members are accessible within the class and by derived classes.

12. What is a virtual function in C++?

Answer: A virtual function is a function defined in a base class and overridden in a derived class. It allows for dynamic (runtime) polymorphism, where the function that gets called depends on the type of object pointed to by a base class pointer.

```
class Base {
public:
    virtual void show() { cout << "Base class"; }
};

class Derived : public Base {
public:
    void show() override { cout << "Derived class"; }
};
```

13. What is the use of const keyword in C++?

Answer: The const keyword defines constants and indicates that a variable's value cannot be changed after initialization. It can also be used to specify that a pointer or reference is constant.

const int MAX = 100;

14. What is operator overloading in C++?

Answer: Operator overloading allows you to define custom behavior for operators when they are used with user-defined types. It helps in creating intuitive syntax for classes.

```
class Complex {
public:
    int real, imag;
    Complex operator + (const Complex& obj) {
        Complex temp;
        temp.real = real + obj.real;
        temp.imag = imag + obj.imag;
        return temp;
    }
};
```

15. What are static members in C++?

Answer: Static members are shared by all objects of the class, rather than each object having its own copy. They are initialized only once and can be accessed without creating an object.

```
class MyClass {
public:
    static int count; // Static member
};
```

16. What is a destructor in C++?

Answer: A destructor is a special member function called when an object is destroyed. It is used to free resources allocated by the object.

```
class MyClass {
public:
    ~MyClass() { cout << "Object destroyed!"; }
};
```

17. What is a template in C++?

Answer: A template is a feature that allows you to write generic code. You can define functions or classes that work with any data type.

```
template <typename T>
T add(T a, T b) { return a + b; }
```

18. What is the difference between new and malloc?

Answer:

- new is an operator that initializes the memory and calls the constructor.
- malloc is a standard library function that allocates memory but doesn't initialize the memory or call constructors.

19. Explain the concept of RAII in C++.

Answer: RAII (Resource Acquisition Is Initialization) is a programming idiom where resources like memory or file handles are tied to the lifetime of objects. When an object goes out of scope, its destructor is called, releasing the resources.

20. What are smart pointers in C++?

Answer: Smart pointers are wrappers around raw pointers that automatically manage memory. Types include unique_ptr, shared_ptr, and weak_ptr, which help in avoiding memory leaks and dangling pointers.

21. What is the difference between struct and class in C++?

Answer:

- In struct, members are public by default.

- In class, members are private by default. Other than that, there's no functional difference between struct and class.

22. What is the purpose of the explicit keyword in C++?

Answer: The explicit keyword is used to prevent implicit conversions or copy-initialization. It ensures that constructors are called explicitly.

```
class MyClass {
public:
   explicit MyClass(int a) { }
};
```

23. What are typedef and using in C++?

Answer: typedef and using are used to create aliases for data types.

- typedef creates an alias for an existing type.
- using is the more modern approach to achieve the same result.

```
typedef int MyInt;
using MyInt = int;
```

24. What is a pure virtual function in C++?

Answer: A pure virtual function is a virtual function with no implementation in the base class. It forces derived classes to implement it, making the base class abstract.

```
class Shape {
public:
    virtual void draw() = 0; // Pure virtual function
};
```

25. What is the use of mutable keyword in C++?

Answer: The mutable keyword allows a member of a class to be modified even if the object is const. It's used to implement members that don't affect the object's logical state.

26. What is the difference between shallow copy and deep copy in C++?

Answer:

- **Shallow copy** copies the values of the data members, and pointers still refer to the same memory.
- **Deep copy** creates a copy of the actual data pointed to by pointers, ensuring that the copied object is independent.

27. Explain the concept of "friend" class in C++.

Answer: A friend class or function can access private and protected members of the class. This is useful when you want to allow specific external functions or classes to manipulate the internals of your class.

28. What is exception handling in C++?

Answer: C++ supports exception handling with try, catch, and throw. It helps in catching runtime errors and handling them gracefully, ensuring that the program does not terminate abruptly.

```
try {
    throw 10;
} catch (int e) {
    cout << "Caught exception: " << e;
}
```

29. What are the benefits of using namespaces in C++?

Answer: Namespaces help avoid name conflicts by grouping related classes, functions, and variables under a unique name. This is especially useful when different libraries might have functions with the same name.

30. What is the difference between std::vector and std::array?

Answer:

- std::array is a fixed-size array, meaning its size cannot be changed after initialization.
- std::vector is a dynamic array, allowing the size to grow or shrink at runtime.

www.ingramcontent.com/pod-product-compliance
Lightning Source LLC
LaVergne TN
LVHW051704050326
832903LV00032B/3997

The book "C++ Essentials: A Pocket Reference" by Debajyoti Bhattacharjee is a concise guide designed for quick reference, catering to both students and educators in the field of programming. This pocket-sized reference book focuses on the essentials of C++ programming, making it an ideal tool for quick look-ups and concept refreshers.

The book distills core C++ topics in a well-organized and accessible manner. It covers fundamental elements like syntax, data types, operators, control structures, and functions, providing a strong foundation for beginners. Additionally, it dives into more complex topics, such as object-oriented programming concepts, including classes, inheritance, polymorphism, and exception handling. This makes it a valuable resource for students aiming to reinforce their understanding or clarify specific points while working on assignments, projects, or studying for exams.

For teachers, "C++ Essentials" serves as a handy tool to support lecture preparation, offering clear explanations and examples that can be directly referenced in the classroom. The compact format allows instructors to address student queries efficiently and provide quick clarifications on programming concepts without delving into lengthy texts.

ISBN 9798345839690

90000

9 798345 839690